A Lesson in
SCHOOL REFORM
from Great Britain

A Lesson in
SCHOOL REFORM
from Great Britain

John E. Chubb
and
Terry M. Moe

The Brookings Institution
Washington, D.C.

About Brookings

The Brookings Institution is a private nonprofit organization devoted to research, education, and publication on important issues of domestic and foreign policy. Its principal purpose is to bring knowledge to bear on the current and emerging policy problems facing the American people.

A board of trustees is responsible for general supervision of the Institution and safeguarding of its independence. The president is the chief administrative officer and bears final responsibility for the decision to publish a manuscript as a Brookings book. Publication of a work signifies that it is deemed a competent treatment worthy of public consideration but does not imply endorsement of conclusions or recommendations. The Institution itself does not take positions on policy issues.

Foreword

PLAGUED BY EDUCATION PROBLEMS that have stubbornly resisted conventional treatment, the United States is now considering radical remedies: a national curriculum with national tests, school-level control of education, and parental choice of schools. These ideas are at the heart of the Bush administration's comprehensive education strategy, America 2000, and the focus of hot debates in the nation's capital and at state and local levels.

Interestingly, a package of reforms very similar to that proposed for the United States began to be implemented in Great Britain in 1988. Indeed, important steps toward these reforms were taken early in the decade. One would think that the British experience would be receiving careful scrutiny by participants in the emerging American debate. So far, it has not.

This study is the beginning of an effort to see what the British experience has to teach. In the summer of 1991, John E. Chubb, a senior fellow at Brookings, and Terry M. Moe, a professor at Stanford University, went to England to observe the effects of Britain's bold educational experiment. With the financial support and scheduling assistance of the *Sunday Times* they visited a wide variety of schools, paying special attention to those in the poor neighborhoods of London and Birmingham. They interviewed teachers and headmasters and obtained reactions from elected officials, administrators, leaders of interest groups, and academics whose views spanned the political spectrum. The first product of this research was an essay published in the *Sunday Times Maga-*

zine on February 9, 1992. This monograph is an expansion of that essay.

The work reported here is ongoing, part of a comprehensive follow-up study to the authors' 1990 book, *Politics, Markets, and America's Schools*. Ordinarily, the Brookings Institution waits until projects are completed and peer reviewed before publishing the results. An exception has been made in this case because the research is unusually timely. Evidence on systemwide school reform is hard to come by. Whether American reformers agree or disagree with the authors' preliminary conclusions, they should find the British experience to be of the utmost relevance to their own efforts at thoroughgoing reform.

The authors wish to acknowledge the support of the *Sunday Times*, especially the encouragement to conduct the enquiry by editor Andrew F. Neil and the tireless help and advice of *Times* education correspondent Charles Hymas. Brookings would like to acknowledge support for the larger project, of which this is an outgrowth, from the Lynde and Harry Bradley Foundation, the Horace W. Goldsmith Foundation, the J. M. Foundation, the John M. Olin Foundation, the Pacific Telesis Foundation, and the Quaker Oats Company. At Brookings, Eric Lawrence provided research assistance and Antoinette Williams word processing. James R. Schneider edited the manuscript.

The views expressed in this study are those of the authors and should not be ascribed to any of the persons or organizations acknowledged above, or to the trustees, officers, or other staff members of the Brookings Institution.

Bruce K. MacLaury
President

February 1992
Washington, D.C.

Contents

Addressing the Problem   6

Choice as a System   9

Why Choice Alone?   11

The Politics of Reform   13

Open Enrollment   17

City Technology Colleges   20

Opting Out   28

Making a Good System Better   41

Prospects for the Future   45

AMERICANS SEE THE BRITISH SCHOOL SYSTEM as a model of academic excellence. They also see it as offensively elitist. The image is one in which most British kids are weeded out at a young age, and only the gifted or economically privileged are allowed to continue. Those in school wear uniforms. They sit in neat rows. They speak only when called upon, and then only in well-constructed paragraphs. They gain an encyclopedic knowledge of literature, history, Latin, and other subjects so necessary to high culture and intellectual discourse. They emerge superbly educated, fit to take up leading positions in British government and society.

As with most stereotypes, there is something to this. But it remains a good distance from the truth, especially now. Americans have probably been watching too many old movies. If our compatriots could travel to Great Britain, as we did, and observe the British schools first-hand, we think they would be struck by how similar these schools are to American schools, at least in basic respects.

The symbols of elitism, the 11-plus exam and the grammar schools, are long gone as foundations of British education. The British state, like the American state, is dedicated to providing all kids with an education, and most of its schools are comprehensives that bring together children of varying ability levels and socioeconomic backgrounds. These schools, like American schools, have plenty of problems and are struggling to do their jobs well. Their kids engage in all the disruptive behaviors that American kids do, including drug use and violence. While some of these kids manage to learn quite a lot, many don't learn much at all. And what they do learn is often irrelevant to the needs of a changing, technologically advanced society. To any American, this is all too familiar.

British schools may be somewhat better than American schools. Tests of international achievement would seem to point in this direction. But this is not saying very much. For American kids routinely score dead last, or nearly so, in the rankings. Anybody can beat the Americans. And British students aren't exactly vying with the Japanese and the Koreans for first place. Their test scores look more like the Americans' than the highflyers', sad to say. Moreover, it has to be pointed out that the vast majority of British schoolkids, bored and turned off, voluntarily drop out before they complete high school. America graduates, and at least minimally educates, a far higher portion of its youth than Britain. And so, for that matter, does every other developed democracy in the West. The dropout rate alone is an indication that something is severely wrong with British education. Kids can't be educated if they aren't even in school.

Poorly educated kids grow up into poorly educated—and unproductive—adults. We are not talking here about an inability to quote from *Hamlet* or do differential calculus without a pencil. We are talking, as British business leaders have been for over a decade now, about a lack of very basic knowledge and skills: about the inability to read, write, or do simple calculations with any real facility. In a recent poll, for instance, a sample of British adults was asked: "If you borrowed £6,000 to buy a car and the flat rate of interest was 12 percent, how much interest would you pay the first year?" Fully 59 percent could not figure out the answer.

The British system is not a model of academic excellence, any more than the American system is. Both have fallen far short of providing children from all walks of life with solid academic training. Both have failed to equip their economies with skilled workers who can be flexible, innovative, and productive in a changing world. And both, for precisely these reasons, have generated widespread dissatisfaction in virtually all quarters—and have become prime targets for political reform.

In the United States, the watershed event was the publication in 1983 of *A Nation at Risk*, the report of a blue-ribbon presidential panel, which argued in grim terms about a "rising tide of mediocrity" in the nation's schools.This quickly generated a powerful movement for change. In state after state, reform packages were soon adopted with great fanfare and high expectations. Education budgets and teacher salaries were dramatically increased, graduation requirements raised, teacher certification standards bolstered, school days lengthened.

But as the 1980s drew to a close, American reformers gradually came to a nearly unanimous conclusion: their efforts had failed to bring about real improvement in America's schools. The causes of ineffective performance appeared to be much more deeply rooted than they had believed, and to require much more fundamental reforms that entail major changes in the traditional system of public education. The movement thus entered a new phase that some call restructuring.

During this phase, three types of reforms have grabbed most of the attention. The first is school-based management, which seeks to decentralize decisionmaking to the school level. The second is choice, which seeks to liberate schools from most governmental controls and make them more responsive to parents and students. The third is accountability, which—especially in light of the greater autonomy afforded schools under the other two reforms—seeks to measure and enforce standards for school performance and thus to ensure that schools do their jobs well. All three, often in combination, are being advocated by reformers in districts and states throughout the country.

A similar story can be told for Britain. There, the initial catalyst for educational change was Prime Minister James Callaghan's

1976 speech at Ruskin College, in which he warned that British schools were failing to prepare the nation's youth for productive lives in a modern, technically sophisticated world. From that point on, education rose on the nation's political agenda, and people all along the ideological spectrum began debating and promoting reform. For the most part, action focused on the same sorts of concerns that initially occupied the Americans: money, standards, qualifications, teaching methods.

But by the latter part of the 1980s, the Thatcher government was ready to push for much bolder, more fundamental reforms. The result was the landmark Education Reform Act of 1988, which in one stroke imposed a radically new institutional framework on British education—a framework built around the same three types of reforms that American activists were pushing for at the time, and still are.

Under the act, power would be decentralized through "local management of schools," another name for what Americans call school-based management. Choice would be enhanced in important ways: by spelling out the rights of parents and students to choose their own schools, by giving schools the right to "opt out" of their local education authorities (LEAs), and by creating new kinds of schools—city technology colleges—for people to choose from. Finally, this population of more autonomous schools would be held accountable through a new national curriculum and a comprehensive battery of tests.

The big difference between British and American educational reform is that the British have been able to legislate in one bold package the kind of thing that Americans can only talk, fight, and dream about. The reason is that the British have a political advantage. Their parliamentary system concentrates authority in the majority party, which, if it has the will, can design radical new programs and simply pass them into law. Under the American system of separation of powers and federalism, authority is fragmented and no one has enough of it to do much of anything.

American reformers find themselves pushing for incremental changes in 50 states and 16,000 school districts around the country, compromising endlessly as they go.

So, while British policymakers readily say that they have long paid attention to American educational reform and tried to learn from it, the fact is that the British themselves, not the Americans, are on the cutting edge of reform. They are the pioneers. Indeed, in terms of the sheer magnitude of the changes it stands to bring about, their 1988 Education Act may well be the most significant educational development in either country during the postwar era.

We went to Britain in the summer of 1991 to get a first-hand look at this revolution in the making, aiming to judge for ourselves whether the 1988 reform has a real chance of succeeding. Is it a stunning blow for a brighter educational future, as its designers claim? Or is it, as many critics argue, really a right-wing conspiracy to bring back the traditionalism and elitism of Britain's educational past? Or might it be a little bit of both—and much more besides?

We didn't arrive with blank slates, of course. We have been studying schools (mainly American schools) for many years, and we came equipped with reasonably well defined views about reform. But we needed to know more. So we conducted interviews with a range of people directly involved—public officials, administrators, school heads, teachers, reform advocates. We also visited a full spectrum of schools around the country—primary and secondary, grammar schools and comprehensives, grant-maintained schools (those that have opted out), voluntary-aided schools (religious schools supported by state money), private schools, single-sex schools.

What we have to say here will probably make no one very happy. Both supporters and opponents of the Education Reform Act will find parts of our argument difficult to swallow. And many of our colleagues in the educational community will be dismayed as well, for our views about reform are quite critical of the establishment. Be that as it may, we hope that readers will find our discussion to be thought-provoking and that, even if we don't win a popularity contest, our ideas will somehow contribute to the creation of better schools. This, in the end, is what counts.

Addressing the Problem

If reforms are to work, they have to attack the underlying causes of the problem. In this case, the basic problem is that the schools are performing poorly. The intellectual task for reformers is to figure out why. What are the causes of poor performance? Only when they have an answer are they in a position to design reforms that genuinely stand to promote better schools.

American reformers have generally not approached their task in this way. Nor, so far as we can tell, have British reformers. They have demanded more spending, stricter standards, account-ability, and all the rest primarily because these reforms are polit-ically acceptable and seem to make good sense. They are obvious ways of improving the schools. There is just one hitch: these things do not attack the underlying causes of ineffective schooling.

One of the most basic findings from education research, for instance, is that there is *no* consistent relationship between spend-ing and educational outcomes. The evidence strongly suggests that money is not the cause of the problem. Yet reformers proceed as though it is, because it seems so obvious that it should be—and because leaders of the educational establishment, who are politi-cally powerful and speak "with authority" on such matters, are quick to say that spending is the key to success. Much the same applies for most other popular reforms: they seem to make good sense, the educational establishment provides intellectual and political support for them—and they don't work. They don't address the causes of the problem.

Our book, *Politics, Markets, and America's Schools*, is best known for its advocacy of school choice. Establishment types—most of whom, we suspect, have never read it—tend to characterize it as some sort of a right-wing diatribe that, in advocating a full-fledged choice system, threatens the end of the civilized world. But those who read the book (and have no stake in mischaracterizing it) will see that virtually the whole thing is really about the question of cause. It is an extensive study, based on the largest comprehensive survey of American schools currently available, that explores the foundations of school performance.

We will spare you the details. But we do want to summarize its basic themes so that you will know where we're coming from. We also want to emphasize that, in almost all respects, what we have to say about schools is not controversial at all and is entirely compatible with mainstream research.

Our basic claim is simply that the organization of schools has a big impact on how much students learn and that the organizations that promote learning best—the ones that are most effectively organized—tend to have certain properties. Among other things, they tend to have strong leadership, clear goals, high expectations, orderly environments, and lots of professionalism. Broadly speaking, they operate like informal, cooperative teams. No controversy here. Everyone agrees that organization matters and that this is what effective schools tend to look like. Indeed, these are the kinds of schools that educators have been trying—with little success—to promote for the last decade.

Under what conditions, then, do effective school organizations tend to take root and prosper? Above all else, schools must have substantial autonomy—or, to put it the other way around, they must be substantially free from bureaucratic control, from externally imposed rules and regulations that tell people in the schools what to do. This is hardly surprising. True professionalism and teamlike organization can only occur when the people involved are given the discretion to exercise their own judgment and are not buried in formal restrictions. Again, reformers and mainstream educators heartily agree with this. Since the mid-1980s their call has consistently been for less bureaucracy and more autonomy.

This brings us to the final step, the point at which we part company with the mainstream. How can school autonomy be nurtured and protected so that schools can develop effective organizations? The answer: except under special circumstances, meaningful autonomy *is not possible* within the current educational system. This educators desperately want to deny.

How can we say such a horrible thing? Think about how the system works. As things now stand, schools are simply part of government: bottom-level subordinates in a hierarchy of democratic authority and control. Their superiors are politicians and administrators of various descriptions, all of whom have authority to tell the schools what to do and how to do it, and all of whom are under constant pressure from constituencies and interest groups of every imaginable type to put that authority to use in controlling the schools. As democratic officials, they have strong incentives to respond to these democratic pressures. And respond they do—with policies, rules, and regulations to which the schools must adhere. The inevitable result, over time, is that the schools get buried in bureaucracy.

This is not due to some sort of malfunction. Nor can it be blamed on the incompetence or ill intentions of the people within it. The fact is, the system works exactly the way it is supposed to work: it controls the schools from above in response to legitimate democratic pressure. When public officials and educators do their jobs and do them well—as, we think, is typically the case—the schools inevitably get bureaucratized and, in the process, denied the foundations of effective organization. Bureaucratic, ineffective schools are simply normal for a system of top-down control.

If reformers want to create a population of effective schools, then, they cannot do so by trying to make the current system "work better." It already works great. Effective organizations can only thrive in a context that grants them substantial autonomy, and the current system is built to deny them that autonomy—this is what it does when it works the way it is supposed to work. The problem of school performance is fundamentally a system problem, and it requires for its solution a new kind of system: a system that nurtures and promotes school autonomy and that gives educators incentives to use their autonomy in the most productive ways.

This is precisely what a choice system does—and why, at the end of our book, we embrace choice as the most promising path to educational reform. Unlike all the other reforms that have attracted attention and support over the past decade, choice attacks the underlying causes of ineffective schooling. It gets to the root of the problem.

Choice as a System

A genuine system of choice can take many forms. But at a minimum it consists of three building blocks. First, parents and students must be granted the right to choose their own schools—to search out the good ones, to abandon the bad ones, and to have their own preferences, interests, and judgments respected. In the vernacular this is often called open enrollment.

Second, they must be given something to choose from. Open enrollment is meaningless if choice is restricted to a fixed set of schools whose numbers and types are predetermined. The supply of schools must be liberated so that new schools of various types can emerge in dynamic response to the needs and interests of students, and so that schools that fail to attract support can go out of business.

Third, all the crucial decisions about organization and governance must be placed in the hands of the schools. They must be truly autonomous. For this to happen, and for it to be real and enduring, the authority to control the schools from above must be eliminated as far as possible. Any authority that remains will inevitably become a magnet for political pressure, and it will eventually be used to reassert control when the schools exercise their autonomy in ways that powerful political interests do not like.

As we see it, choice is by no means a free market approach to education. It is a *governmental* system, just as the current one is. It is simply built to provide education in a different, more productive way—through a new governmental structure that does most of its work through markets rather than politics and bureaucracy. The government's job is not to abandon the schools but to *use* markets to see that the schools flourish and prosper as effective organizations.

The standard criticisms of choice are aimed at the free market. They argue that people are not well enough informed to make good choices; that people need transportation if choice is to be meaningful; that schools will discriminate in admissions; that segregation problems will get worse; that hate groups and other undesirables will set up schools; that schools will go out of business and leave students in the lurch; and so on. And because these problems are most likely to afflict the poor and minorities, they say, a choice system would push these people into second-class schools (or worse), denying them any semblance of equal educational opportunity, while the middle and upper-middle classes make out like bandits.

These are valid concerns, and they point to problems that may certainly plague a free market. But choice is not a free market system. Its educational markets operate within an institutional framework, and the government's job is to design the framework so that these concerns are dealt with. Among other things, this might involve setting and administering rules for the chartering of new schools; seeing that information is provided (through personal contact) to all parents; setting up rules for the applications and admissions processes to ensure that choice is open and fair; setting up rules and providing additional funding to ensure equal opportunity for kids with serious disadvantages; and providing transportation to those that need it.

If this framework is designed with care and concern, markets can be allowed to work their wonders within it—for everyone's benefit. Schools will have the autonomy and the incentives to develop effective organizations and to specialize their programs to meet the diverse needs of parents and students from all walks of life. New schools will emerge to meet unmet needs, some of them offering innovative approaches to education that no public official or planner could ever have dreamed up. And some schools—bad at what they do, perhaps, or innovative in unpopular ways—will die out, as they should. The result is a system stacked in favor of effective schools. And stacked in favor of providing people—all people, regardless of income or ethnicity or disabilities—with the kinds of schools they want. Markets, operating within the right institutional framework, can do this. Top-down control cannot.

Why Choice Alone?

Now let's take a look at the other two reforms occupying center stage in Britain and the United States: local management of schools and accountability. Do they get to the root of the problem of school performance?

Local management of schools is a good idea, as far as it goes, because it seeks to enhance school autonomy. But it does this by keeping the traditional top-down system intact and decentralizing certain budgetary and decisionmaking authority to the school level. Bureaucracy remains a problem—there are plenty of rules, for instance, that limit school autonomy and specify exactly how and when it is to be exercised. More important, the hierarchy of authority remains, full of politicians and administrators eager to expand their dominion over the schools and subject to all sorts of pressure from constituents and social groups who want schools to do their bidding. These pressures are always a threat, but they are especially strong from groups unhappy with how the schools are actually using their autonomy. In this kind of system, the schools are only safe from political attack and control when they do not use their autonomy to strike out on their own. This is not, and can never be, true autonomy.

It is tempting to think that local management of schools is a nice complement to choice and that the two make sense as a package. But a true choice system actually makes LMS superfluous. For schools of choice are entirely autonomous, and they run their own affairs as they see fit. They don't need LMS. The notion that the two make a nice package is reasonable only when the top-down system is maintained and a few elements of choice—rather than a choice system—are to be introduced. But, to put it mildly, this is far from ideal. Choice can do everything LMS can do and a great deal more. When choice is taken seriously, LMS is beside the point.

Accountability helps ensure that school performance can be measured, monitored, and channeled toward desirable social goals. If it is done right, this can be valuable. But the approach to accountability that has captured the minds of American and British reformers leaves the top-down system unchanged. Indeed, it is itself a top-down reform and actually reduces school autonomy by placing new power in the hands of the authorities (and the test designers). This new power allows them to impose all sorts of new constraints on teachers and students—what should be taught, how it should be taught, and how much time these things should take up. It also allows them to use their evaluations of schools as bases for control: for sorting the bad from the good and taking action from above to turn the bad ones around. While some form of accountability is necessary in any system, the approach of modern reformers leaves the underlying causes of poor performance untouched, and even stands to make things worse.

Within a choice system, the main form of accountability is bottom-up, a concept foreign to bureaucrats and politicians. School quality is in the hands of teachers, school heads, and governing boards, who make their own decisions about everything that matters. Parents and students, free to choose, then pass judgment on how well the schools are doing in providing the types and quality of services they want. They support schools that please them. They abandon schools that don't. This is how schools are held accountable—by the power and decisions of the people they serve.

Top-down accountability mechanisms still have a role in a choice system. Society has a stake in ensuring that basic social values are upheld and that important social goals are pursued. It also has a stake in knowing how well the schools are doing in promoting these sorts of outcomes. A national curriculum, a system of tests, and, indeed, the basic institutional framework for education are all means of doing this. The crucial caveat—which in today's politics is almost always violated—is that these things must not be highly constraining. The schools must be free to chart their own course, and it is parents and students—not the state—that have the primary role in holding the schools accountable. If the state assumes this role, accountability threatens to become a facade for ever-mounting political and bureaucratic control.

The Politics of Reform

So far, we have mainly talked about the ideas behind reform—about what works, what doesn't work, and why. This is what might be called the intellectual side of reform. There is another side, however, that is actually far more important in determining what kinds of reforms get adopted—the political side. Here, good ideas can get embraced. Or ignored or corrupted or compromised away. And bad ideas, or simply ideas that will not work, can prove highly popular and durable.

For educational reform arises out of politics, and politics is driven by power. It is serious business, the stakes are high, and the most powerful players—public officials, party leaders, leaders of organized interests—tend to have very diverse views of what ought to be done. These views are only partly based on ideas about cause and effect. More often, and more fundamentally, they are anchored in vested interests and ideology. The battle is waged under the banner of school improvement, but for many players there is much more involved than that.

In the United States, for example, the single most powerful force in the politics of education is the National Education Association, a union that represents some 2 million teachers nationwide. One does not have to comb the education research literature on the causes of school performance to figure out what the NEA's position on choice is. It opposes choice with maniacal fervor. Is this because choice won't work? That is what the NEA says, of course.

But the fact is, choice is the ultimate threat to NEA interests: it would destroy an educational system that grants the union special power and privilege. The NEA does not want that. Period. Exactly the same applies for the other established groups in American educational politics—school boards, administrators, superintendents, education schools, and so on. Right down the line, the people who speak "with authority" on education are against choice. It is the reform they fear most, their worst nightmare.

In the politics of restructuring, as a result, the three major reform proposals—local management of schools, choice, and accountability—have met with very different responses from the powers that be. Local management of schools and accountability have generated controversy simply because they call for genuine changes—changes in authority, changes in the ways things are done. But both leave the system intact, and because they do, they have proven acceptable to many members of the establishment.

The details are often bitterly fought over, but the basic approaches have garnered widespread support. In cities and states around the country, political forces have been coalescing behind some combination of school-based management and accountability.

Choice is in another league. Because the idea that people should have the right to choose their own schools is highly popular among ordinary citizens, leaders of the establishment are quick to say that they "support choice." But what this means, in practice, is that they are willing to consider setting up magnet schools or perhaps some form of open enrollment within the framework of the traditional top-down system. When reform groups push for a true choice system, one that would liberate the supply of schools and do away with most top-down authority, the establishment drops its facade of support and prepares for war, unleashing its formidable political weapons to keep choice from making inroads. The most brutal and deeply rooted conflicts in American education reform are over choice, not over school-based management or accountability.

The unfortunate fact, then, is that the single reform that promises to work is precisely the one that is most strenuously resisted by established interests—and the least likely, therefore, to be adopted. The reforms most likely to gain support and be adopted are reforms that do *not* get to the root of the problem. The success of American school reform turns on the extent to which this dilemma can be overcome.

In British politics, the basic patterns are similar. Local management of schools, for instance, was resisted by the Labour party and much of the educational establishment, particularly the local education authorities, because the devolution of authority to the schools reduced their own power. But the system remained intact. The LEAs continued to perform many of their traditional educational functions, Labour maintained its power base in the LEAs, and both remained an integral part of the larger control structure. While there was much controversy over the idea of local management of schools in the beginning, it increasingly became a battle over details—with everyone essentially agreeing that local management of schools was a worthy reform. At this writing, Labour claims that, were it to take the reins of national power again, it would leave local mangement in place.

The idea of a national curriculum and testing program generated lots of controversy in the beginning as well. Teachers resisted because they did not want to be straitjacketed in the classroom. LEAs resisted because they did not want to lose their traditional role in setting the curriculum. And Labour, which controls many LEAs, suspected that this was a conservative plot to eliminate its influence over what gets taught in the schools. But again, as the relevant commissions were set up and specific action taken, the controversy eventually came to focus on the details. What exactly would the national curriculum look like? How would the tests be constructed, who would administer them, and how? The basic thrust of reform was soon not a matter of controversy at all. All the major players came to agree that a national curriculum with testing was a good idea.

But choice has proven very different. As we noted, the Education Reform Act promotes choice in three basic ways: open enrollment, opting out, and the creation of city technology colleges. The least controversial of these is open enrollment, which, as in the United States, can readily be incorporated into the top-down system. It is an administrative headache but not a disaster. Opting out is another matter. Under this provision, the act allows schools to leave the authority of the LEAs entirely and become "grant-maintained"—accountable only to their governing boards and the national government. This is a truly radical reform of the system that threatens to remove schools from most (existing) political control, overthrow established interests, and put most educational administrators out of jobs. Not surprisingly, the establishment and its Labour allies have not warmed to opting out. They are just as opposed to it today as they were in 1988. Unlike the other reforms,

opting out threatens the very foundations of the system. Labour has clearly indicated that, were it to gain national power, the opting-out provision would be voided and all grant-maintained schools would be forced back into their LEAs.

Much the same is true for the city technology colleges, but on a smaller scale. The idea here was to create twenty new schools, funded in part by private donations from business, that would offer a combination of academic and vocational-technical training, thus providing an education that, for some kids, would be more relevant to their future lives, more conducive to gainful employment, and simply more interesting. This too is an antisystem reform. It loosens the LEAs' iron grip on the supply of schools, allowing new schools to emerge without their consent. An important role in the location, design, and staffing of these new schools would be played by the private sector—which, to the establishment, is absolutely unacceptable. And these schools would be on their own, outside LEA control, competing with the mainstream LEA schools for students—successfully, no doubt. To protectors of the system, this is a nightmare come true. Thus, Labour and the establishment have been crusaders against the city technology colleges from the beginning, and their opposition continues unabated.

In Britain as in the United States, then, local management of schools and accountability are the preferred approaches to radical educational reform. But they are preferred because they are not really radical. They leave the system in place, and they are not that threatening. Only choice is radical—in concept, at least—because it is the only one that targets the system. This is why choice, and choice alone, is anathema to the powers that be. And why it faces such an uphill battle.

Open Enrollment

Let's take a closer look, now, at the three choice provisions of the Education Reform Act. What kinds of changes have they wrought so far? Do they seem to be working? What are their likely consequences for the future?

The starting point for any choice-based reform is open enrollment: parents and students must be allowed to select their own schools. This is where the Conservatives started, and well before the 1988 act. They first included a Charter of Parents' Rights in their platform for the 1974 election and, upon capturing the helm of government in 1979, set about fashioning new legislation to introduce choice into British education.

The 1980 act was an incremental reform. Among other things, it directed the LEAs to honor parental preferences, to set up local appeals procedures for parents dissatisfied with the results, and to provide parents with test results and other information relevant to their choice of schools. But it also contained a huge loophole: LEAs were not bound to honor parent requests that would "prejudice the provision of efficient education or the efficient use of resources." In practice, then, the local authorities were free to allocate kids pretty much as they wanted—and, of course, they did. They declared popular schools to be full even when additional space remained. They funneled overflow children into unpopular schools to maintain attendance levels and economic viability. They moved kids around to achieve academic or ethnic (or whatever) balances they regarded as good.

The 1988 Education Reform Act was an explicit attempt to make choice more meaningful by reducing the LEAs' power to interfere. No longer would they be allowed to circumvent parental choice by claiming priority for administrative concerns. The only justification would now be the physical capacity of the school, a "standard number" of places determined at the national level. LEAs were required to admit students to popular schools up to (and sometimes beyond) their standard numbers, even if that meant that unpopular schools would be left with many places unfilled. For the most part, this has had the desired effect: the LEAs are less capable of interfering, and power has clearly shifted to parents.

In our view, the British experience with school choice has been a very positive one. Ordinary people, many of them uncomfortable at first with their new decisionmaking role, came to like it—and, after a short time, to expect and demand it. Whereas choice used to be regarded as an educational experiment of sorts, it is now becoming the norm and is taking on the status of a perceived right. As Donald Naismith, chief educational officer of the Wandsworth LEA puts it, "The argument is won. People like and want choice. Having experienced it for some years now, they are addicted to it. There is no going back."

Before choice became so popular and entrenched, Labour and establishment opponents were quick to assert that parents are unfit to make such awesomely complex decisions, that they are too ill-informed and too little motivated by factors of genuine relevance to their kids' education. The fact is, these decisions really aren't complex at all. And research on how parents have exercised choice during the 1980s has shown that this patronizing view of parents is unwarranted.

Now that parents are no longer told what to do but are empowered to make choices of real consequence for their children, they are reaching out to get informed about the schools available to them—visiting schools personally, comparing prospectuses, talking with friends and community members, paying attention to school reputations. And what are they looking for in a school? Great sports teams? Attractive uniforms? Hardly. Desmond Nuttal, director of research for the Inner London Education Authority during the late 1980s, puts it this way: "Parents have taken choice very seriously, and research has shown great consistency in what they tend to be looking for: they want order and discipline, academic achievement, and proximity." In other words, the typical parent is seeking out the best possible school close to home.

Based on our interviews with school heads, it is clear that parental choice—and the funding that follows it—has bred a heightened sensitivity to pleasing the client. Heads whose schools are oversubscribed are quick to acknowledge it; they are proud of it; and they explain it by pointing to the quality of their programs, staffs, and learning environments. Heads whose schools are under-subscribed are defensive and embarrassed—and eager to claim that changes are under way to attract more students. While, in the past, success was measured by how well the school pleased its LEA superiors, this is no longer enough or even necessary. Because of choice, success is now crucially dependent on pleasing parents, and the schools are doing what they can (which is not always much, given the constraints) to make themselves attractive. Increasingly, this is the way they seem to think about their jobs.

On the whole, then, open enrollment has worked quite well, as far as it goes. But its beneficial effects are limited by the top-down system into which it has been inserted. The system does its best to smother it. LEAs continue to have substantial authority and discretion, and they still take action to assert their own priorities over those of parents. Kids still get allocated. Bad schools still get rewarded with students and funds they do not deserve. Schools still get closed or merged or changed in character—and choices elim-inated. And Labour, given half a chance, would still take action to see choice—which, as an obviously popular reform, it now public-ly "supports"—subordinated to the myriad requirements of ad-ministrative control.

City Technology Colleges

The most glaring deficiency of the 1988 Education Reform Act is that it does almost nothing to liberate the supply of schools. For all practical purposes, the numbers and types of schools are fixed: they are the same as they were before the act took effect. It grants people choice, but gives them little that is genuinely new to choose from—failing to set forces in motion that would generate a broader, more diverse range of quality schools.

There is one exception: the city technology colleges. This is a dimension of the act that many would now say is dead. Private funding has proven more difficult to come by than the government initially hoped, and only thirteen CTCs are currently operating, to be followed in the near future by two more. That could be the end of it. Faced with surplus capacity in the rest of the system, financial pressures to cut back, and withering criticism from Labour and the establishment, the government has indicated it has no intention of building more.

We have our own reasons for thinking that the CTC strategy was ill advised. So why talk about it at all? The reason is that it exemplifies some of the most important strengths and weaknesses of the act.

The CTCs inject new life and expanded choice into a calcified British school system. The LEAs are closing schools, not creating new ones. And they are standardizing and homogenizing the schools under their control, not encouraging difference and diversity and daring innovation. The CTCs may well be a drop in the bucket, but they are a very special drop indeed.

The CTCs speak directly to some of the most critical problems in British education. They are built especially for poor and working-class kids in urban areas, often in the blighted inner cities. These are the kids who most desperately need help and whose own schools are failing them most miserably. They are trapped in a bleak world with no future, and the CTCs offer them a way out—and an extraordinarily attractive one at that. It is no accident that urban kids are beating a path to their doors, and that all the existing CTCs are hugely oversubscribed—with, on the average, three times more applicants than places.

The kind of education the CTCs offer is precisely the sort that Prime Minister Callaghan appealed for long ago: an education that is directly relevant to the economic lives and productivity of British youth and the economic well-being of the nation. The CTC program combines academics and vocational training, is closely linked—through both subject matter and work-related experiences—with industry, and gives special emphasis to mathematics, science, and technology, including the most recent developments in computers and information processing. This is also the kind of balanced, diverse curriculum that has a special appeal to urban kids, many of whom are turned off by pure academics and are especially interested in gaining technical proficiency and work-related skills of value in a modern, fast-paced economy. The CTC curriculum is tailor-made for keeping these kids in school, teaching them something useful, and reversing the serious dropout problem that has long plagued the British system.

A standard line from critics is that the CTCs are selective, that they skim the cream by taking the best students. But this is not true in any meaningful sense. Because the CTCs are so popular, they cannot admit everyone—and they are indeed careful about whom they admit: they want students who are motivated to learn, who have a special interest in what the CTCs have to offer, and whose parents are committed to being involved and supportive. This has nothing to do with class, ethnicity, or other bases of social stratification. It has to do with the unique qualities of individual kids and their parents, and how well they match up with those of the school. The CTC ethos is one of hard work and high expectations—for everyone. Indeed, they keep their kids in class more hours a week (five) and more days a year (fifteen) than the state-maintained schools. They seek out students—almost all of them economically disadvantaged—who are up to the challenge. This is the kind of selectivity that is good and productive.

As organizations, the CTCs are free of LEA control, and the whole idea is for them to use their autonomy to develop the programs, staffing, curricula, and relationships most conducive to effective schooling. They have every opportunity to strike out in imaginative new directions, to do what works and abandon what does not. School heads are expected to be genuine leaders in all this—not managers or administrators—taking entrepreneurial action in fashioning a truly productive school. Bureaucracy from above is not a factor. And bureaucracy from within—as a mode of internal school organization—is definitely out. The CTC philosophy puts the emphasis on flexibility, self-reliance, and teamwork: which, for teachers, can only be a liberating contrast to the routines and hassles of working in a state-maintained school. Not surprisingly, teachers are flocking to the CTCs. According to Cyril Taylor, chair of the CTC Fund, they recently had some 2,000 applicants for 50 advertised jobs. This while the establishment talks of teacher shortages.

To learn more about the CTCs first-hand, we visited the Kingshurst CTC in Solihul, which opened its doors in September 1988 as Britain's first CTC. We were impressed with what we saw. Its head, Valerie Bragg, was given virtually carte blanche by her governing board and the Department of Education and Science to develop a good school from scratch. She began with a run-down building acquired from the Solihul LEA, and she renovated it in truly stunning fashion. The colors are varied and bright; there are lots of open spaces and social areas to encourage interaction; rooms are divided in unorthodox ways; furniture comes in odd shapes and sizes; decor changes from room to room. Just being in the building is an interesting, even exciting experience. The key to all this was not money, but autonomy and ideas: Bragg has a keen interest in interior design, knows what kind of physical environment she wants to create for her students, and has the freedom to make her ideas reality. No need to choose from the LEA catalog.

In staffing, too, she has had virtually a free hand, unconstrained by unions, bureaucracy, and politics. And she has used it creatively. "Formal certification is unnecessary, and other formal qualifications are often irrelevant to whether people can teach. I try to elicit innovative types. I want people who have flair, who can get on with others, who have the ability to communicate. With teaching, you can either do it or you can't."

Relationships among teachers, and between teachers and administrators, are kept as informal as possible. "The staff work in teams," she says, "and the notion of a team is central to how this school operates." Indeed, things are so informal that teachers are not the only ones who teach. The support staff also teach within what is called the enrichment program, which includes activities ranging from aerobics to learning about reptiles. Even the caretaker has a teaching role: he used to be in the army, and he teaches students about camouflaging, among other things. This, in fact, is part of her calculus in hiring everybody—what can they contribute to the students? No one is just a secretary or just a caretaker.

The kids are expected to work hard, and discipline is well observed. The place is incredibly orderly. At the same time, however, there is lots of interaction and movement and free expression. This is part of the school's ethos: students work independently, at their own pace, and are accorded "complete freedom and trust"—the rooms within the school are never locked, for instance, and are always available to them. For this to work, the students clearly have to be properly motivated and socialized, and this is a big part of the school's job, especially for the new arrivals. One simple way that this is accomplished: everybody eats breakfast together every morning. In Bragg's words, "it is a community affair"—it builds personal bonds, understanding, and an acceptance of the norms that knit all members of the school together.

Who are these kids? They are, to begin with, very lucky. The school is located in a low-income urban area, and the vast majority of all kids in its catchment area apply for admission—only to be turned down for lack of space. This past year, according to Bragg, the school had 1,000 applications for 180 first-year slots. This is the clearest sign that something of great value is going on here: everyone wants in. They want to go here instead of their local LEA school.

This very popularity forces the school to be selective in admissions. Elitism has nothing to do with it. Quite the contrary.

By law (and CTC philosophy) kids are drawn from all ability levels, not just the brightest. In addition, Bragg looks for the motivation to learn, and she makes a special effort to include kids who are minorities, who come from deprived backgrounds, or who are disabled. So the students that get admitted are hardly the crème de la crème, whatever that might mean. They are just ordinary working-class and poor kids, representative of the Solihul-Birmingham area, many of whom would doubtless be problems in other schools and eventually drop out. But not here. Kingshurst kids come to school every day; average attendance is a remarkable 96 percent, compared to about 50 percent in the surrounding LEA schools. And some 80 percent of these kids are staying on until the age of eighteen, compared to a dismal 20 percent in the state schools. Something special is happening at Kingshurst—to regular kids.

What pulls all these elements—from the design of the building to the development of staff and programs to the admission and socialization of kids—into a coherent whole that has all the earmarks of effective organization? The explanation is not money. Despite what critics might say, Kingshurst has roughly the same operating budget (determined mainly by per-child allotments) that LEA schools get. The best explanation, it appears, is leadership—and the autonomy that makes it possible. For Bragg, who used to be head at a large, well-respected comprehensive school, leadership is clearly the key, and she is far better able to lead at Kingshurst than she was in the state system. "This place has much more potential. Here, I can do things at the click of a finger. . . . All you really need is someone who can lead."

This is a rosy picture. What, then, could possibly be wrong with it? Why did we say earlier that we had reservations about the CTC strategy of educational reform? The fact is, there is nothing wrong with the picture. The Kingshurst CTC appears to be a wonderful, highly effective school. An enviable achievement. And there is good reason to suspect that the other CTCs are probably much like it, born as they are of the same basic elements. But when this whole approach to school reform is entertained as a matter of broad national policy, the picture begins to get a lot bigger—and it is not quite so rosy.

There are three problems. First, there are not enough CTCs to make much of a difference, and it is unrealistic to expect much increase in their numbers down the road. Each one costs about £10 million to create. While this is the normal amount the DES would expect to spend in creating any state school—the CTCs are not advantaged in this respect, as critics claim—the fact is the DES and local governments are not creating new schools. They are closing schools, eliminating surplus places, and trying to save money. In this environment, building lots of CTCs at £10 million a pop is not exactly a political winner. And building just a few of them cannot do the job.

Second, while the CTCs appear to be money well spent, the fact is that new schools can provide kids with good educations at much lower cost. It takes teachers, books, rented (or donated) space, and not a great deal more. The notion that new schools cost £10 million is a major misconception that prevents policymakers from expanding the supply of schools—and expanding choice.

Third, and most important, the CTC approach to innovation and liberation of the supply side is inherently limited. The point of the CTCs is to create new types of schools that fill a gap in the existing system. They cater to important needs and interests that are currently going unmet, and they cater to them in a distinctive, productive way. This is why they are so popular. But, as a matter of policy, is this the best way to inject innovative new schools into the system, so that the supply of schools is responsive to what people want? We don't think so.

Ultimately, the CTC approach to innovation and supply is really typical of the way these matters have always been approached within education. They are approached from the top down. People in high positions come up with ideas about what needs and interests are important, how they should be addressed through schools of a certain type, and how much all this presumably costs (which is invariably a fortune); and the schools are then imposed from above. As a general strategy, this is hopelessly inadequate. The types of schools it generates (if any) are subject to all the usual political influences from powerful players, who have their own agendas and interests at heart. And even if the supply of schools could magically be left up to "objective" policymakers on high, they could never know enough—about what people want, about the diverse schools needed to satisfy them—to do the job well.

One thing is for sure. People are different, and, if given half a chance, would seek out all sorts of educational options. Some would want schools that emphasize mathematics, science, and technology, as the CTCs do. But others would prefer schools that specialize in the performing arts, or the humanities, or the social sciences, or foreign languages. And this is just the beginning. For there are countless aspects of schools that people value—and that different people value differently—when given the choice. Some like schools that are small and personal, while others like the diversity and expanded curricular offerings of a large school. Some are especially concerned with academic rigor, while others place more emphasis on social development and a nurturing environment. Some want single-sex schools (especially for their daughters), while others believe that coeducational schools are healthier. We could go on, endlessly.

The best way to see that people get the kinds of schools they really want is not to tell planners to come up with good ideas from above. It is to set up an institutional framework that allows new schools to emerge of their own accord, to allow them to decide for themselves what services they will offer and how they will be organized and staffed—and then to let parents choose among them. The schools that actually tap into the needs and interests of parents, and that do so effectively and at low cost, will succeed. The others will not, and will leave the scene. These forces—

market forces operating within a governmental framework—
promote a diverse population of schools that do a far better job of
matching the diverse wants of parents than central planners ever
could and that build on creative energies and innovative ideas that
far outstrip anything top-down control could hope to produce.

Opting Out

Opting out is the truly revolutionary idea put forward by the
1988 act. Open enrollment is severely compromised by the system.
The CTCs are too few to make a real difference, and they are top-
down innovations. But opting out attacks the system head-on,
allowing schools to leave their LEAs and move out on their own,
taking students, money, and all relevant decisionmaking power
with them. In their new status as grant-maintained schools, they
are still subject to top-down control by the DES. But for now, at
least, the DES is not inclined to exercise it—and they enjoy almost
total freedom. If enough schools were to follow this path, the
existing system would collapse and a very new and different one
would take its place—a system whose hallmark is the foundation
of effective education: school autonomy.

At this writing, about 100 schools have gone through the
legally prescribed steps—beginning with votes by parents and
governing boards and ending with approval of formal proposals by
the DES—to achieve grant-maintained status. Another 140 or so
have announced their intention to opt out and are at various stages
of the process. These schools are the pioneers. The uncertainties
are daunting, the political pressures formidable. But they are doing
it anyway. And their experiences—and successes—are fast providing models for other schools to emulate. By almost all accounts,
even the accounts of the most savage critics, this hesitant early
response from just a tiny percentage of Britain's some 33,000
schools is but the beginning of a widespread rush to opt out.

What kinds of schools are opting out, and why? A common theme struck by critics is that schools are opting out not for the autonomy but because they are threatened by closure or change of character by their LEAs and want to prevent their own demise. This motivation is portrayed as somehow illegitimate, with grammar schools, single-sex schools, and boarding schools—the vestiges of elitism, according to the Left—allowed to escape from the advancing forces of progressivism.

That such an exodus should be occurring, especially at the earliest stage, is not surprising, nor in our view is it a bad thing. It is a very good thing. They are fleeing the oppressive political decisions of public authorities, and there is no reason whatever to think that these authorities know best and ought to prevail. Schools that leave still have to attract support from parents and students, and this is the real test of whether they ought to remain in existence and keep their character.

A look at the data on opting out suggests the stereotype so highly publicized by critics is not the essence of the process anyway. Schools threatened with closure or change account for only 35 percent or so of the total thus far. Moreover, the schools facing such pressure tended to act right away. As time has gone by, fewer and fewer of the schools seeking grant-maintained status have done so for these reasons. Increasingly, all sorts of schools are trying to opt out. It is happening everywhere, in more than half the LEAs in the country so far, in poor areas as well as rich.

What are the inducements for opting out? Our interviews with school heads clearly suggest that the two major inducements are autonomy and money, which are closely bound up with one another. Critics like to say that, aside from the schools that are simply escaping, the driving motivation is really just money. The grant-maintained schools get a per-child allowance, just as LEA schools do under local management of schools; but they also get an extra amount, roughly equal to their share of LEA administrative costs—an amount the LEA loses. So grant-motivated schools get more operating funds than the LEA schools do. About 16 percent more, on the average. The trade-off is that they do not receive LEA administrative services—inspection, curriculum development, teacher training, psychological counseling, and the like—unless they specifically contract and pay for them.

But money cannot be separated from autonomy. By giving the GM schools their share of administrative expenses, the government empowers them to make their own decisions—autonomous decisions—about a whole range of issues that were previously decided by the LEAs. This is not, in point of fact, extra money. It is money that was always there and, in some sense, was always being spent on the schools—but not necessarily in ways the schools wanted or valued. Now, the GM schools decide how the money will be spent, while the rest of the schools have these decisions made for them by their LEAs. It's an autonomy issue.

The heads of GM schools do not put much value on LEA services, so they do not see themselves as giving up much. More generally, they are frustrated by what they see as a bloated administrative system, unresponsive and ineffective. In the words of Cecil Knight, head of Small Heath School in Birmingham, "I miss the LEA's services very little. This LEA is a bad, inefficient, slow bureaucracy, insensitive to the needs of the inner city." And what does he do for services now? Some he didn't want in the first place. Those he does want—advisory services, for instance—he now purchases elsewhere.

Roger Perks, head of the Baverstock School, has a similar attitude. He didn't value LEA services at all, he says, and found himself continually stymied in trying to build a better school for his kids. "The straw that broke the camel's back came when the LEA rejected—for the fifth time—our request to fix a bad leak in the school's roof. This was sheer neglect." After opting out, Perks used his new autonomy and money to work all sorts of wonders at Baverstock. Among other things, he got the roof repaired—right away, through a supplier of his own choosing, at a cost of £1,700.

The LEA estimate had been £35,000.

Much the same sort of story, interestingly enough, is told by John McIntosh, head of the London Oratory School. This is a voluntary-aided school affiliated with the Catholic Church that, as such, enjoyed somewhat greater latitude under its LEA than the regular schools do. But even for a voluntary-aided school, political control is substantial. The LEA determines the numbers of teachers and nonteachers, salaries, allowances for books and equipments, funds for repairs; and it provides the usual range of services the school may not value. McIntosh found all this counterproductive. "The LEA represents a tier of bureaucracy that is quite unnecessary. It absorbs a disproportionate share of the resources. And I found myself spending a disproportionate amount of my time dealing with it. I wanted full autonomy."

It is no surprise to find that the heads of schools that have opted out are down on the system. That is why they left. But what about the heads of state schools that remain within the system? What do they think of their LEAs? Do they think about opting out?

Current school heads rose to their jobs under the existing system, and they are not, by and large, a revolutionary lot. Most of the people we talked to seemed to be dedicated to their work, to fit comfortably within the LEA hierarchy, to believe in the system—and yet virtually all expressed frustration with how slow and cumbersome it is, and with how little value their own school gets out of it. A typical observation comes from Dick Cooper, head of the Fircroft Primary School in Wandsworth: "I don't place much value on LEA services, and I am convinced I could do quite well on my own. But I like being part of a system, and I see no compelling reason to break out."

Support for the system among school heads appears to be tepid and abstract. They often like the idea—it's the reality that bothers them. But at least for now, it does not bother them enough to justify taking on the burdens, uncertainties, and political conflicts associated with opting out. This applies across a full range of schools. The head of one comprehensive secondary school in a working-class section of London, for example, claimed that she would never opt out because she believes strongly in the system. What she did not say is that her school probably could not make it on the outside anyway: it is vastly undersubscribed, managing to fill just 600 of its 1,000 seats, and then only because the LEA allocates students to the school who haven't chosen it. Opting out would be suicide. At the other extreme is a grammar school for girls in Kingston that has everything going for it: a select, highly motivated student body, high exam scores, a great reputation, and a Conservative LEA that protects it. The head of this school is not interested in opting out. Why rock the boat?

There seem to be plenty within the state system, however, that yearn to get out. One of these is the head of a comprehensive secondary school in perhaps the toughest area of London, an area plagued by poverty, drugs, and prostitution. His brand of leadership is forceful, hands-on, and all-encompassing, and he says he has succeeded in creating a school that, while still awash in serious problems, is "friendly and nonviolent—which is nothing short of a miracle in this environment." The choice-indicator backs him up: this year, the school has received 230 requests for only 180 places. He is doing something right.

He is also fed up with his LEA. He says it is filled with inexperienced, incompetent people—people he identified by name and whose backgrounds he knew in detail—who flatly do not know enough to be helpful to him, who are unresponsive to the school's simplest needs (for painting and window repair, for instance), and who burden him with ridiculous bureaucratic requirements that make his already difficult job virtually impossible. "If I request an advertisement for a teaching job," he complains, "it takes weeks to appear, if it appears at all, and then it is published first in ethnic journals rather than in papers that would stimulate a wide range of applications. I can lose whole terms this way." He also has horror stories that go beyond the merely inefficient. His

LEA, he says, sent out paychecks to his former employees for months (and in one case, a full year) after they had left; more than a million pounds in bad checks were mailed out before he was finally able to stop the madness.

He thinks his school would be far better off outside the system. "I certainly don't need the LEA," he says. "All I want is the money, and I'll run everything myself. If it was down to me, I'd opt out." It is not, however, down to him. He needs the support of his governing board, and its members are currently undecided: about half are leaning toward opting out, but they are worried about the possibility of a Labour victory in the next election, which would torpedo all their efforts. So, for now, they wait to see what politics has in store for them.

Politics. For schools throughout Britain, this has been the major impediment to reform. The simple promise that a Labour government would eliminate opting out has had a chilling effect all by itself. But to put the lid on even more securely, Labour and the establishment have organized concerted attacks from the very beginning to make opting out as costly and uncertain as possible for schools that may be considering it, even when those schools are serving people who are their traditional constituents and allies, and whose interests they supposedly represent and protect. Their heated opposition ensures—as it is supposed to ensure—that the decision to opt out cannot be what the Education Reform Act intends for it to be: a judgment by parents about what is best for the quality of their school and the education of their kids. Instead, the very discussion of opting out is a political act, and a dangerous one.

This shows up in the aggregate statistics. More than twice as many ballots to opt out have occurred in Conservative than in Labour LEAs, even though some 60 percent of all schools are located in the latter. When opting-out activity does occur in Labour LEAs, it is more likely to be driven by desperation—by threatened closure or change of character—than it is in Conservative LEAs, where the environment is less hostile and it can arise more naturally. Of all schools balloting to opt out in Labour LEAs, 45 percent did so because they were under such threats, whereas the corresponding figure for Conservative LEAs is only 29 percent.

Specifically, what does this resistance to opting out look like? One of the most egregious cases is that of Small Heath, which was among the first schools to consider opting out in 1989. Small Heath serves an immigrant population, most of them Muslims with roots in Pakistan and Bangladesh. While unemployment and illiteracy are high among its people, family bonds are strong, and they place a great emphasis on education as their key to a better future.

As we noted earlier, the school head, Cecil Knight, had little use for the Birmingham LEA. He was confident that he could run the school much more efficiently and provide far better facilities and services for his kids if he were free from LEA control and able to spend the money as he saw fit. Having led the school ably for five years, and having a well-deserved reputation for valuing and respecting multiculturalism—indeed, in 1987 he was awarded the Order of the British Empire for his contribution to the city's multicultural religious program—Knight had the strong support of the governing board. When the Education Reform Act came along, he saw opting out as the opportunity he had been waiting for. He convinced the governing board to follow his lead, and they in turn mobilized support among the parents.

After declaring its intention to opt out, the school began preparing for a vote on the issue. Conservatives at the national and local levels were enthusiastic in their support. But the Labour-controlled LEA, prominent Labourites, and union leaders—the traditional allies of the poor in British politics—began sharpening their knives to prevent the Small Heath community from running its own school. A group of Labour members of parliament presaged the coming holocaust by proclaiming, "The head teacher and governors should be in no doubt that their proposals are matters of major political concern in the neighborhood and will have to be vigorously resisted. We very much regret that a major controversy will arise, which their irresponsibility will have created."

Soon, all hell broke loose. Establishment forces used every tactic imaginable—and the public's money—to influence the election and its outcome. They went to court to prevent a vote from taking place. Parents were buried in leaflets implying all sorts of undesirable consequences—that most teachers would quit, that school meals would be discontinued—and even offering bribes (volunteering to begin providing "halal meat . . . for children whose religion and culture require it"). Establishment armies went door-to-door explaining the horrors of opting out and urging parents to vote no. Cecil Knight was the target of sleazy but well-publicized attacks on his character, including charges that, of all things, he was anti-Muslim and unfit to educate Small Heath kids. And when, despite it all, parents voted to opt out anyway, the establishment raised legal challenges on every conceivable issue, seeking to have the entire vote thrown out.

In the end, the establishment lost. And Small Heath, after a long, bloody battle with their traditional "friends," was finally granted its autonomy as a grant-maintained school. But in the grander scheme of things, this was not really the end. It was the beginning of a new educational world in which schools were free to opt out. And while the establishment may have lost the battle, it had struck a blow for victory in the larger war: all schools were now on warning that what had happened to Small Heath could happen to them. They would have to think twice about opting out.

If schools are to venture down this path, then, the inducements we singled out earlier—autonomy and money—will often be insufficient. Schools may find opting out enormously attractive, yet do nothing about it. As the Small Heath case serves to illustrate, another key ingredient must usually be present if they are to take action: they must have strong leaders who want to take charge, who are unafraid of political conflict, and who can convince their governing boards and parents that opting out will succeed. While on paper the governing boards and the parents are supposed to be the prime movers in all this, the reality is that they lack expertise and experience and are often easily intimidated by the establishment. They need strong leadership if they are to be galvanized into action—and it is the school heads who must usually provide it.

What do schools actually do with their autonomy if and when they get it? Are they in fact capable of handling all the responsibilities that autonomy thrusts upon them, and will they exercise their new freedom in ways that promote quality education for the full spectrum of British kids? The critics like to claim that autonomy generates serious problems on both counts. It overburdens schools and prevents them from performing effectively because they really do need what the larger system provides. And it promotes social inequality because it allows schools to move toward a more elitist, class-based education.

What does the evidence suggest so far? Perhaps the first point to make is that, placed in the right hands, autonomy is quite manageable. Most school heads are eminently capable of running their schools all by themselves, without help from above. Roger Perks of Baverstock quickly rejected any suggestion that his school was somehow hard to run. "It's a piece of cake. There's no mystique in it at all." Cecil Knight of Small Heath was of the same mind. "I personally don't find it at all difficult. It's the most natural thing in the world." Like Valery Bragg, head of the Kingshurst CTC, they simply did not regard autonomy as a burden. They assumed their responsibilities easily—and eagerly. As Perks put it, "As soon as I read the Reform Act, the adrenalin started flowing."

The heads of LEA schools are more diverse, more system oriented, and do not have the same measure of autonomy. But their experiences under local management of schools (LMS) are quite relevant here. While some complained to us about the increased workload caused by LMS, all were enthusiastic about the increased control it gave them over everything from programs to staffing to repairs, and all wanted to keep the new powers and responsibilities they had gained. Like the heads of grant-maintained schools, they rejected the notion that autonomy was too burdensome or complicated for them to handle. While we heard stories about heads who quit their jobs rather than shoulder the new work—turnover that is both inevitable and healthy—the people we talked to were excited and empowered by LMS.

A good example is Robert Brunning, head of the Churchill Gardens primary school in London. Here was a man who expressed undying affection for the now-defunct Inner London Education Authority, support for the system, and antipathy for the Conservative government. Yet, when given the opportunity under LMS to control his own funds, he quickly became an entrepreneur. Among other things, he used his new authority to eliminate the traditional ILEA arrangement for caretakers, whereby they were paid a set salary, provided with free housing on the premises, and obliged to perform specific tasks in return. He hired a new caretaker for £5,000 less a year and wrote up a job description that requires him to do "three times as much." The house is no longer part of the deal: Brunning intends to rent it out and use the money for his school. Overall, he believes he is using his new autonomy to real advantage under LMS, and he wants to keep it.

Much of the publicity surrounding autonomy has focused on this sort of entrepreneurialism and its consequences for the schools' facilities, staffs, and resources. Especially in the grant-maintained schools, which have far more autonomy than LMS allows, these consequences are often dramatic and far-reaching. At Small Heath, for instance, Knight has added five new teachers, an artist-in-residence, a new music room with new instruments (music wasn't offered before), a new business studies suite with computers, new books, new paint and repairs, machines for working with wood and plastic, subsidized trips abroad, trips to galleries and museums, and a new satellite dish to provide Asian language programs (recall that the school is 90 percent Asian).

These sorts of things are important, of course, and graphically demonstrate what strong leaders can do for their schools when they, rather than LEA officials, are making decisions about how to allocate education funds. But still, the most crucial aspects of schooling and school reform have to do with its human side: with the kinds of people inside the school, with how they relate to one another, and generally with the school's ethos. And the school heads are well aware of this. As Roger Perks observed, "I turned this school around by changing the relationships within it, not by changing the buildings and facilities."

Baverstock, he says is a "community school." Its climate is "happy and caring," but also traditional: the students wear uniforms, attend daily religious assemblies, and are taught the value of self-discipline and proper manners. The mix obviously works, and Perks is its personification—exuding traditional values, yet wandering the halls embracing children, engaging them in easy conversation, showing unique concern for each of them, and through his unbounded enthusiasm, inspiring them.

Such a clear sense of mission arises from autonomy and the full rein it gives to leadership. But school heads cannot succeed alone. Above all else, they need to recruit able teachers who share the school's mission and can support its ethos. Before opting out, Perks claims, he had a hard time attracting good people. But now, precisely because opting out has proved so successful at Baverstock, he is deluged by applicants. Teachers, much to the consternation of unions and the establishment, are eager to work at grant-maintained schools: they like the resources, they like the freedom. An advertised job may yield between 50 and 100 applications. And Perks chooses carefully: "I only appoint people who absolutely burn to teach." And people, clearly, who fit well into the kind of community he is trying to build.

Compare this to the experience of the head of a state comprehensive in Fulham. With recruitment highly constrained by the LEA and firing a virtual impossibility, the composition and character of the staff are largely beyond his control. Many clearly do not share his ideas about schooling. He believes, for instance, that gifted kids—like the disadvantaged—can benefit from special teaching methods and curricula. Which, of course, is quite true. But when he brought in a speaker to address his staff on the matter, he recounts, "they attacked her. There was nearly a riot. Many of my teachers are very ideological—egalitarian—and they see me as an elitist." With such diversity and conflict literally imposed from without, there is obviously no chance for a shared sense of mission to develop within. Indeed, when asked what his school's ethos was, he replied with a wry smile, "controlled chaos."

The GM schools do not have to put up with all this. They are free to recruit the kinds of people and build the kinds of organizations that they want. But who are the children that actually benefit, in the final analysis? Do the grant-maintained schools use their autonomy to provide ordinary kids with a better education, or do they escape from "progressive" controls in order to pursue elitism and exclusivity, as their critics claim?

As far as we can tell, the story here is very much like that of the CTCs: the schools serve ordinary kids, and they serve them better. Small Heath serves a population of poor immigrants, and since going grant-maintained, it has used its autonomy to build the kind of school that these people want for themselves. It is very much a product of its community. When choice was first instituted, Small Heath lost some of the local kids to schools in more affluent Birmingham neighborhoods; but since it achieved GM status, the exodus has turned around. One of Knight's primary goals has been to serve his local community so well that all its kids want to come to Small Heath.

Baverstock does not have the unifying Muslim culture that envelops Small Heath. It is located in a low-income, high-crime part of town, and because of its popularity as a GM school—this year it received 530 applicants for 240 slots—it has had every opportunity to pull away from its "undesirable" local community and accept more advantaged students from further away. But it has not done this. By design, virtually all kids who get accepted live within a mile or so of the school.

In part, this is a reflection of Perks's own philosophy. He believes in taking care of his own patch. But it is also a matter of school strategy and mission. Baverstock has built its success on parental involvement and community support. The school is open four nights a week for various community events, including opportunities for adult education. Much of the sprucing up has been done by parent volunteers, who have formed painting parties and garden groups. And vandalism, due to the vigilance of loyal residents in the vicinity, is way down. In Perks's view, rejecting local kids is unthinkable—and unwise. The key to success lies in finding better ways to serve them.

Finally, consider the London Oratory School, which has always been selective in its admissions. On the surface, it appears to have all the earmarks of an elitist institution: squeeky-clean kids, full uniforms, emaculate facilities. But who are these kids? Most are working class, many from Spanish, Italian, or Portuguese families. They are drawn from all ability levels. And some 800 of its 1,200 pupils commute to the school, often by subway, from all over London. These kids and their parents—ordinary people by class-based standards—are the London Oratory School's community. They are highly motivated, they want the kind of education the school provides—with an emphasis on Catholic values, academic excellence, and strict discipline—and the school's success turns on pleasing them. Going grant-maintained hasn't changed anything. And there is certainly nothing elitist about ordinary people getting the kind of education they want.

We cannot claim, of course, to have comprehensive knowledge of grant-maintained schools. But everything we have seen suggests that opting out works extremely well when it is in capable hands. From what we can tell, school heads do not find complete autonomy a burden—and, far from missing the experts allegedly so crucial to the education process, feel empowered when allowed to go their own way. They put their autonomy to good use in building better schools—hiring good people, creating a shared mission and ethos, beefing up facilities, adding new subjects and services, seeking out cost-effective ways of doing things. And throughout, they were clearly catering to the needs and interests of parents, students, and their local communities—regardless of class, regardless of ethnicity—well aware that, in an environment of choice, pleasing them is the key to success.

Making a Good System Better

We heard a consistent theme again and again during our interviews, even from school heads who are sympathetic to the traditional top-down system. The next election, they all agree, will determine the future of British education. If Labour wins, the opting-out experiment is over and the traditional system will be pieced together again. But if the Conservatives win, there will be a stampede to opt out. While many schools may hold back, what is left of the LEA structure will be so weakened that there will be increasingly little reason for the remaining state schools to stay within it—and they, too, will begin to leave. As one head of an LEA school put it, "If the Conservatives win, it will be exceptional not to opt out."

Should the Conservatives win, moreover, they would presumably be in power for years to come, and the GM schools would then have ample opportunity to dig in—to cultivate parent and community support, to develop networks of relationships, to solidify their organizations. They would become entrenched as part of the institutional landscape. Were Labour to reassume power someday, it would find that reality had passed it by, and that powerful vested interests were arrayed against any major change in the new system of grant-maintained schools. The positions would be reversed, and Labour would find it difficult or impossible to reinstall the ancien régime. And politically unwise, in all likelihood, to try.

The result of all this—assuming it continues—will be something that closely resembles a full-blown choice system. Through open enrollment, parents and students will have the right to choose their own schools. And as opting out proceeds, there will be a growing population of autonomous schools to choose from, schools that are forced to compete with one another for parent and student support. We have no doubt that a system built largely on these foundations—choice, autonomy, competition—would provide British kids from all walks of life with better schools and better educations than the old system ever could.

The Education Reform Act is a stunning achievement, and reforms of this magnitude are rare. So, on practical grounds at least, there is little sense in complaining that it does not go far enough. But we must emphasize, as we did earlier, that the act has all but ignored a basic requirement of a well-functioning choice system: the liberation of the supply of schools. As things now stand, parents are forced to choose among the existing schools— which severely limits their educational options, limits competition among schools, and fails to take advantage of the great power of markets in generating diversity and innovation. If choice is to work as well as it can in serving the wide range of educational needs and interests within the population, there must be some mechanism to allow for the emergence of new schools from below. This is absolutely crucial. Failing to recognize this is the act's Achilles' heel.

There are several ways of addressing this problem, all of them at least somewhere within the realm of political feasibility. The first is that new schools, upon meeting certain standards, could be allowed to "opt in" to the new state system. They would thus become grant-maintained and qualify for public funding on the same basis as other schools. Legislation along these general lines has in fact been introduced into the House of Lords by Lady Caroline Cox.

Existing private schools are the most obvious candidates for opting in. Many of these schools are quite good, and they represent an array of choices that, for financial reasons, are beyond the reach of most parents. If they were allowed to opt in, many might find it attractive to become part of the state system—and this would vastly expand the choices available to everyone, as well as increase competition among the state schools. Our preference, we should say, is to require all such schools to be free, and thus equally accessible to everyone regardless of class; tuition-charging schools would remain private.

More generally, any qualifying group or individual might be allowed to set up new schools and opt in. Groups of teachers in the state schools, for instance, might be encouraged to hive off and form their own schools—built around special programs or staff skills, let's say—and so qualify for GM status and state funds. (This, by the way, is essentially how East Harlem, New York, created its very successful choice system. It relied on its teachers.) Businesses, unions, educational experts, or churches might do the same. The possibilities are endless. The point of all this is not to privatize the public system, as critics always contend, but rather to build a bigger, more dynamic, more diverse state system. There would be lots more schools of all different shapes and sizes and specialties—all playing by the same democratic rules of the game.

A second way of expanding the supply of state schools is for government to allow more schools to become voluntary-aided. As a result of a deal struck between government and religious author-ities long ago, certain religious schools—almost every one of them either Catholic or Anglican—have been placed under LEA control (less restrictive than for other state schools) and granted state funding. This option has rarely extended to other religions. There is no justification for this kind of favoritism, as far as we can see. All the major religious groups—including the Muslims and others who are different from the British mainstream—deserve to be treated equally. If they were, this too would add new numbers and dynamism to the state system. This would especially be beneficial, of course, if the voluntary-aided schools were liberated from LEA authority and made grant-maintained instead.

Third, the government should allow grant-maintained schools to change their character at will. The Education Reform Act required GM schools to keep their original character, and it set up a procedure for changing it that put the ultimate decision in the hands of the secretary of state. This, apparently, was a protection against schools' using their freedom to become elitist. But there is nothing to fear in this regard, and there is much to lose—in responsiveness, in diversity, in innovation—by placing undue restrictions on what GM schools can become. If these schools are to serve the mass of British citizens, they must be given the autonomy to grow, develop, and change as they see fit.

Fourth, the government could help free up the supply of schools if it would stop closing and consolidating schools to eliminate surplus places—and use these places instead to provide the flexibility and capacity to accommodate lots of new schools. It is important to realize that a building and a school are not the same thing: more than one school—and schools of different sizes and types—can occupy any given building. The fact that Britain has surplus places, therefore, opens up all sorts of innovative possibilities. When people have ideas for new schools, or when they want to expand or multiply existing schools, there is already empty space to put them. Their new schools do not require new buildings or the horrendous costs of constructing them. Schools can be set up, as Lady Cox phrases it, "on faith and a shoestring"—and the closer this is to the truth, the more schools there will be. The government's job is to provide a context that is as friendly and accommodating as possible. The way to do this is to safeguard a certain amount of slack in the system and make it available to new schools.

Which brings us to our fifth and final point about liberating the supply side: the LEAs must be legally prevented from interfering with the emergence of new schools, with the fair and equal allocation of space, and, indeed, with the process of reform as a whole. The behavior of LEAs thus far has been nothing short of outrageous. They have a clear interest, particularly if Labour-controlled, to obstruct the successful operation of the new system, and that is precisely what they have been doing—with the public's money. The government has the authority to put a decisive end to this, and it should take forceful action. (At this writing, Prime Minister John Major appears to be moving in this direction.)

More generally, if the Education Reform Act is to achieve its full potential, the government must recognize that the system it is creating is not really a coherent system. It is a hybrid, a cross between top-down control and choice. If choice is to work to best advantage, the vestiges of top-down control must be eliminated, and a serious effort made to design and install an institutional framework that unleashes the power of choice.

This means, above all else, introducing legal reforms that liberate the supply side. But there is more. It also means addressing the sorts of free market problems we discussed earlier: problems of information, transportation, segregation, equity, and the like. A real choice system, for instance, would not simply force LEAs to make test scores and other information about schools public. It would tackle the information problem more aggressively—by, for instance, setting up government choice offices in each locality that collect information on each school, provide it personally to each parent, and see that they are carefully assisted through each step of the applications and admissions processes. The Education Reform Act doesn't give choice the institutional foundation it needs to do its best work.

Prospects for the Future

Largely because of its experiment in opting out, Britain has already broken with tradition and moved boldly toward a choice-based system of public education. But what are the chances that it can take the additional steps necessary to transcend the traditional system entirely, consolidate choice, and complete the revolution? We have no illusions about this. In the end, educational reform is an intensely political process—and politics is no basis for glorious optimism.

Labour is a lost cause when it comes to educational reform. Labourites are firmly allied with the teachers' unions and other members of the educational establishment. They think of the top-down system, its bureaucracy, and its personnel virtually as their own property and as an integral part of their political legacy to the nation. And they are committed to an ideology of social engineering and political control, in which the schools are vehicles for transmitting politically correct values to British young people.

The whole world is being swept by a realization that markets have tremendous advantages over central control and bureaucracy. But the Labour party is not part of this. Trapped by its own past, it has become a defender of the status quo and a purveyor of old, hopelessly outdated ideas. Yesterday's radical has become today's conservative: resisting change, ignoring new ideas, reliving an era that no longer exists. Markets and choice are elitist. The Education Reform Act is a right-wing conspiracy to revoke the great victory of 1944. These things must be fought if the common man is to be served.

The great irony is that the common man is the real victim of the traditional system. People with money do quite well. They can move to the suburbs in search of good schools or pay for private schools. But most ordinary people in the inner cities, especially the poor and minorities, are stuck. The system provides them with lousy schools, and they have nowhere to go. They are the ones with no choice, the big losers—and so they revolt and demand what the more privileged already have. When they do, however, Labour turns on them in order to protect the system. The party "represents" their interests by fighting and opposing them.

How, then, would Labour go about upgrading British education? Their most recent proposal, announced with great fanfare by Jack Straw, shadow education secretary, is for a more aggressive bureaucracy. "The fundamental flaw in the government's approach," he says, "is to believe that markets can be a substitute for good management. They cannot be." Labour would set target objectives for the nation's schools and back them up by creating a new Education Standards Commission, which would direct both national and LEA inspectorates, subject the schools to more intensive monitoring and evaluation, and intervene when necessary. This does not deserve to be called a reform. It is more of the same from a party that appears incapable, politically and ideologically, of offering anything different.

The Conservatives are another matter. They are not wedded to the bureaucratic status quo, nor are they politically allied with the establishment. The "neoliberal" ideology of markets, minimal government regulation, diversity, and individual freedom is strong within the party. And they are not social engineers intent on using their control over the schools to indoctrinate young people. So it is hardly surprising that it was the Conservatives who designed the Education Reform Act. While often portrayed as old-fashioned— which they are in some respects—they are the only major party capable of making innovative breaks with the past.

This does not mean, however, that the Conservatives can be counted upon to complete the revolution they began. Electorally, this is new turf for them—education has historically been Labour's issue, not theirs—and they are still feeling their way along. A common observation, often made by Tories themselves, is that too many of them—especially those coming out of the independent and grammar schools—are out of touch with state education. This is obviously changing. The party has grabbed the education issue for its own, and some of its leaders are intensely interested and knowledgeable. But it remains, for many, unfamiliar territory.

More familiar are the financial concerns that have always

topped the Conservatives' agenda. But these have gotten in the way of choice-based education reform. Driven to save money and promote efficiency, and faced with surplus places in the schools, the Conservatives have given LEAs strong incentives to close and consolidate schools—and this has limited rather than expanded the educational options of parents. As Wandsworth's Donald Naismith explains, "Despite the rhetoric of Conservatives about choice, their administrative and financial arrangements make such a program virtually impossible."

There are also, we must add, ideological strains within the party that work against choice. Most obviously, some within the party are neoconservatives who strive for a return to traditional British values and institutions, including a more selective (and perhaps more elitist) educational system. They support markets when markets can be made to promote these ends, but otherwise they do not.

There is also an implicit but pernicious ideology of business managerialism that infects the thinking of many throughout the party, even those who see themselves as strong advocates of choice. Their image of efficiency is one of a corporate hierarchy in which things are competently managed. When social problems arise, their automatic response is to think of an administrative solution. Given this mind-set, they are only too comfortable thinking of choice as part of a top-down apparatus, rather than as a radical new system wholly incompatible with it.

So the Conservatives are not knights in shining armor. They took on the bureaucratic behemoth in education, but they didn't finish it off, and they didn't really fashion a coherent new system to take its place. The reasons have to do, in part, with the stiff opposition they faced from Labour and the establishment. But they also have to do with forces internal to the Conservative party itself—for, opposition aside, its leading members simply lacked the ideological commitment and political drive to establish a genuine choice system in education.

Even if the Conservatives go into a holding pattern, the natural dynamics of opting out will transform the top-down system into a hybrid with lots of choice, competition, and autonomy. But will they really go into a holding pattern, or will they overcome their own reservations and try to go all the way? No one can predict this with any confidence. We do think, however, that there is one political wild card in all this that augurs well for renewed Conservative interest in revolution.

The wild card is that a full-blown choice system is most desperately needed by—and bestows disproportionate benefits upon—the poor and minorities in urban areas. These, of course, are traditional Labour constituencies, but Labour cannot and will not respond to their demands for choice. This opens up a political opportunity of the first magnitude for the Conservatives: by aggressively pursuing choice-based reforms, they can forge an alliance with a large and enormously important Labour constituency—and Labour can do nothing about it. The incentives are obvious and the coalition a winner, with the political force to set and carry out its own educational agenda. In our view, this could well be the wave of the future in British educational politics. If so, greater choice is the wave of the future too.

We began this discussion by pointing to similarities between British and American schools, their problems, and the attempts to reform them. We want to end by emphasizing that the similarities actually go much deeper than this. The fact is, virtually everything we have said here about the politics of British education applies straight across the board to the politics of American education. Only the names have to be changed.

In our country, it is the Democrats who are the lost causes: wedded to the educational bureaucracy, forced into pitched battles with the poor, incapable of supporting genuine change. It is the Republicans who represent the only real hope—battling the establishment, promoting choice, weighing in on the side of the poor. The progressives have become conservatives, the conservatives progressives. And the wave of the future? A growing alliance between the Republicans and the urban poor, constructed on their shared belief that choice is the key to better schools in the inner city.

In fundamental respects, then, Britain is not unique. What is happening there is happening in the United States: the problems, the reforms, the conflicts, and the alliances are all roughly the same. The only real difference is that Britain, owing to its parliamentary form of government, has been able to move farther and faster toward a radical overhaul of its educational system—and is far more likely to succeed. We can only hope it does, and that America can someday follow in Britain's footsteps.

DATE DUE
